Who Goes Moo?

A ZEBRA BOOK
By Sue Tarsky
Illustrated by Deborah Ward

PUBLISHED BY
WALKER BOOKS
LONDON

Who quacks?
Who roars?
Who goes oink?

Who croaks?
Who goes moo?
Who goes woof?

Who is big?
Who is the biggest?

Who is small?
Who is the smallest?

Who has hands?
Who has horns?
Who has a shell?

Who has feathers?
Who has sharp teeth?
Who has fur?

Who has wings?
Who has a curly tail?
Who has a shiny black nose?

Who has a hump?
Who has big ears?
Who has a baby in her pouch?

Who has a beak?
Who has a long neck?

Who runs fast?
Who creeps slowly?

Who is standing still?
Who is curled up?

Who is jumping?

Who is standing on the bank?
Who is swimming?
Who is leaping?

Who drinks milk?
Who pecks corn?

Who nibbles cheese?
Who eats a banana?

Which cat would be a good pet?
Which cat has long hair?
Which cat has stripes?
Which cat has spots?

Which babies and mothers belong together?

What is funny about these animals?

goat

pig

cow

hen

snake